DO IT
AFRAID

Do It Afraid

Copyright © 2017 Roxanne Potter. All rights reserved.

No rights claimed for public domain material, all rights reserved. No parts of this publication may be reproduced, stored in any retrieval system, or transmitted in any form or by any means, electronic, mechanical, recording, or otherwise, without the prior written permission of the author. Violations may be subject to civil or criminal penalties.

Unless otherwise marked, all Scripture quotations are from:

KJV – King James Version
NKJV – New King James Version
NIV – New International Version

Library of Congress Control Number: 2017942193

ISBN: 978-1-63308-271-7 (paperback)
        978-1-63308-270-0 (ebook)

Interior and Cover Design by *R'tor John D. Maghuyop*
Cover Photo of Roxanne: *Victor McCune Photography*

CHALFANT ECKERT
PUBLISHING

1028 S Bishop Avenue, Dept. 178
Rolla, MO 65401

Printed in United States of America

DO IT AFRAID

ROXANNE POTTER

CHALFANT ECKERT

PUBLISHING

TABLE OF CONTENTS

Foreword 7

Acknowledgements 9

Introduction 11

Chapter 1:   *Do It Afraid* 15

Chapter 2:   *I Can't Do It!* 25

Chapter 3:   *To Know Him is to Have Faith* 35

Chapter 4:   *Row, Row, Row Your Boat!* 43

Chapter 5:   *Praise Is a Weapon – Use it!* 51

Chapter 6:   *Battle Buddies* 63

Chapter 7:   *Winning! The Battle is in the Mind* 71

A Testimony: Sara Toma 77

About the Author 79

FOREWORD

Roxanne Potter challenges us and charges us to Do It Afraid. This book will inform you and inspire you to walk by faith in the face of fear and failure. It takes courage to do what has never been done. It takes courage to go where others never have gone. Anyone anywhere that ever accomplished anything had to do it afraid. No matter where you are now in life, this book gives you a place to start.

Bishop Ron Webb
Senior Pastor, Mount Calvary Powerhouse Church
Author of *Leadership from Behind the Scenes, Destroying the Root of Racism*, and *Exposing the Enemy from Behind the Scenes*

What a powerful testimony this book is for all that read it. It will enlighten you on being completely dependent on God. Roxanne Potter is very transparent about what God has done in her life. That is exactly what is needed for us to truly grasp the power and love of God in our lives. This book will change your life and give you the faith you need to make it through as well and just like Roxanne does, use your experiences to inspire others to keep trusting God no matter what you face. Roxanne Potter has accomplished the ability to inspire others by being transparent as she trusts God. She writes in a way that will captivate your heart and compel you to trust God.

Evangelist, Bonita Quinn
Author of *No More Bondage* and *You Got What It Takes*

ACKNOWLEDGEMENTS

I want to thank my husband and children for never doubting that God was going to bring me out. I want to thank My Team: JoAnna, Mindy, Tracy, Steve, Jon, Shannon, and Jandale. You all never missed a beat. Your love and faith kept me going.

To all of my many friends who encouraged me daily to remain in the fight.

To my mom: I know you were watching from heaven cheering me on. I learned from you how to fight this battle from the best, you!

And to all the cancer warriors out there. The battle is real. We are strong and we are resilient. We will continue to kick cancer's tail. Warrior on my friends. Never quit and know that God is fighting this battle.

INTRODUCTION

Have you ever been afraid to do something but you knew that you needed to do it?

    Afraid to go the doctor, so you ignore?
    Afraid to change jobs, so you stay?
    Afraid to take a step out in ministry, so you remain unfulfilled?
    Afraid of heartbreak, so you never commit to a relationship?
    Afraid of another church hurt, so you stay home?
    Afraid to get back on that horse, so you quit?
    Afraid to change your diet, so you remain unhealthy?
    Afraid to stop that addiction, so you remain addicted?
    Afraid to wear that new dress, so it stays in the closet?
    Afraid to ask for advice, so you remain lost and confused?
    Afraid to ask for forgiveness, so you remain tortured in your mind?
    Afraid to confront that offense, so you remain offended?

These are just a few of the thousands of "afraid" things we face in our lives that we just don't want to deal with because we are afraid.

I was diagnosed with Stage 3 Triple Negative Breast Cancer in August 2016. In December 2015, I broke my neck in a horse-riding accident. In February of that year, I noticed that I had a new lump on my breast. It wasn't like the normal ones I would get; it was firm and immovable. I didn't think much about it at first, but I noticed it getting bigger. By May of that year, I developed a knot under my armpit that started to hurt. I knew I needed to go to the doctor. I was due for my yearly mammogram, but fear crept over me. I waited until August to finally go to the doctor. Know why? I was afraid. I was driving home one day, and the Lord said to me as clear as day, "Go to the doctor tomorrow and don't push this off anymore." I went to the doctor that next day "afraid."

My surgeon told me that it was possible that I had cancer but it was dormant, and that my neck injury sparked the aggressive spread of the cancer. I often wonder if the fight with cancer would have been as hard if I had gone to the doctor as soon as I realized something was not right. I believe it would have been easier. But fear kept me bound to the unknown, thinking that was a safe place, when in reality it was going to kill me. I thank God that I was able to hear His voice clearly and went to the doctor when I did. It saved my life.

Sometimes we are afraid of what we will find out, or we fear rejection or failure, so we stay put and remain in the darkness. We say spiritual things like, "I will just believe God, it will be okay," but we don't really believe that. It is a crafty trick of the devil. We need to be free from fear, and the best way to do that is to *Do It Afraid*.

> *My people are destroyed for a lack of knowledge…*
> Hosea 4:6 KJV

We are dying spiritually and physically because we refuse to gain knowledge of a situation. We remain trapped in the unknown thinking we are safe there, all the while the devil is stealing from us. Jesus is light. Knowledge brings forth light. Once I found out what I was dealing with, I was able to fight the battle accordingly, and God removed my fear and built my faith. If you never confront what you are afraid of, it will always be your master, and it will always control you.

In this book, I share my experience with breast cancer and how I did not allow it to have me. I conquered it with God's help. My prayer is that as you read this book, you will find tips and tools to help you overcome fear and be equipped in whatever battle that you may be facing. God is always there and is fighting for you to get to the other side. Keep pushing, keep praising, keep speaking the Word, and finally, rest. God gives us the courage and strength to face the things that we are afraid of.

CHAPTER 1

DO IT AFRAID

*Fear not, for I am with you; Be not dismayed,
for I am your God.
I will strengthen you, Yes, I will help you,
I will uphold you with My righteous right hand.*

Isaiah 41:10 NKJV

In the Bible, we see all kinds of examples of heroes that did it afraid. In Exodus 3 and 4, we see that Moses was afraid to leave behind his life in Midian to answer God's call to go back to Egypt and confront Pharaoh to free the Israelites. But we see that he did what God asked of him, and he did it afraid.

In Judges 6 and 7, we read about Gideon who was hiding in a hole because he was afraid. He was so afraid that when God asked him to take down the idols that were built in the village, he waited until dark of night out of fear. The next day the villagers come to Gideon's house, and Gideon hid while his father convinced them not to kill his son. But later we read that the angel of the Lord called Gideon a mighty warrior. A mighty warrior? This was the man that hid in a hole, obeyed God in the dead of night, and needed Dad to protect him. I like this because it shows that even amid our fears, God sees the mighty warrior inside us.

In Joshua 2, we read about Rahab the harlot. Many things can be said about Rahab. However, what I want to point out is that she hid Jewish spies knowing that her life was on the line. Yet with a calm demeanor, she met the ones searching for the spies and sent them out on a false trail. She betrayed her own country, and because of that, she could have been punished by death. I cannot help but admire her courage and her faith. She did it afraid, and because of her faithfulness, Rehab and her whole family were saved.

In Esther, we read of a young woman with the odds against her. Yet even though she was afraid for her life, she faced her fear and entered the King's court knowing that he had the right to have her killed. Her courage saved the Jewish nation.

In I Samuel 17, David faced a giant of a challenge: Goliath was literally a giant and David was a young man. But even though he was afraid, he managed to find the courage within to face his fear of the mighty and overwhelming giant. He trusted God, and he killed Goliath with a slingshot and a stone between the giant's eyes.

The Bible is full of accounts of people who through exercising courage became heroes of the faith. They faced their fears and walked through battles and storms to accomplish greatness and they did it afraid. We can be encouraged when we read about these great people. It should give us hope that with the Lord's help, we can face whatever life throws at us.

At some point in our lives, we have all faced something that caused us to be fearful. I know something about doing it afraid. The phone rang, and I hesitated to answer it. I knew the doctor was on the other line and she was calling with the results of my biopsy.

"Hello," I said.

"Mrs. Potter? How are you today?"

I wanted to just hang the phone up and not deal with it. But I stayed on the phone. She began to share with me the results of my biopsy and ended with, "I am very sorry, but you do have cancer."

I politely said, "Thank you," and set the phone down. Everything that I thought and everything that I knew was about to change.

I walked into the kitchen and called for my husband. I looked at him with complete and utter fear and shock, and said, "I have cancer. I don't think I can do this." As the words slipped off my tongue, I began to pass out and fall to the floor, and my husband caught me. How in the world did this happen to me? How was I going to tell my children? We had just lost my mom to cancer, and now I was going to have to ride this storm out, too. I never felt so scared and alone in all my life as I did in that moment. I went to my room, laid on my bed, and cried.

My appointment to see my surgeon wasn't for another week. The torture of the *unknowing* was almost unbearable. I had to take something because I could not sleep. My anxiety was off the chart. I wanted to hide from the entire world. I wanted to pull the covers over my head and wake up when it was over. Darkness overwhelmed me. I googled everything I could about breast cancer even though I had no idea what stage I was in, if it had spread, or what was going to happen. I caused myself to have all kinds of fear. All I knew was that I had cancer and I was afraid.

It seemed like an eternity before I saw my surgeon. Finally, the day came, and as I sat there waiting for him to come into the room, I stared at the chart on the wall trying to self-diagnose what stage of cancer I had. Then the door opened and there stood the man who held in his hands the storm that was coming at me. He examined me, then he started to explain to me all the details of my report.

He said, "The type of breast cancer you have does not respond to hormone therapy. You have Triple Negative Stage 3 Breast Cancer."

I just stared at him and thought, "No, that cannot be."

He went on to say, "Ten to fifteen percent of all breast cancer is triple negative. Out of the 10-15%, it is predominantly found in African-American women."

Great! I thought. Of all the things I would inherit, I get that? For real?

He went on to say, "Before we can go any further, we need to make sure it has not spread throughout your body, so I am scheduling a CAT/PT right away."

I looked point blank at him and said, "Doctor, am I going to die?"

He looked at me somewhat teary eyed and said, "I want to share this with you. One of the nurse's moms here at the office was diagnosed with Stage 4. She is a lot older than you. She lived for over six years." He said that she had to fight along the way, but she still lived longer than she was supposed to.

He went on to say, "You are young and healthy, and we are going to fight this as aggressively as we can."

I said with tears in my eyes, "Okay, what do we do next?"

At that moment, I realized that I was literally in a battle for my life. He went over what we would do next and honestly, I was so overwhelmed I just wanted to get out of there. I was so afraid. I was angry and disappointed. I got in my car and cried.

I said, "God, I don't want to die. I don't want the same fate as my mother. Show me how to get through this. There has to be something more to this." I continued, "God, I understand breast cancer, but why the most aggressive form and why Stage 3?"

It was in that moment I heard the Spirit of the Lord say as clearly as a perfect sunny day, "Because the bigger the battle, the bigger the testimony and the more glory I receive."

I sighed and thought, "Okay, I can do this. I will live and not die. God, you must have a plan." I am not saying that God gave me cancer. God is not the author of sickness and disease, and I had to settle that in my mind, and you need to settle that in yours.

When you are hit with a word like *cancer*, there is an immediate attack on your mind. Cancer has a demonic force attached to it, and it intends to steal your will to live. That is why you cannot grow weary in the fight. The bigger the diagnosis, the bigger the battle and the more you must fight. But there is a name that is so much bigger than cancer, and that is the name of Jesus Christ.

Any battle you face will require a warrior mentality. You cannot enter a battle weak or already defeated. You must enter the battle prepared to warrior up and fight. You must put on your armor.

Put on the whole armour of God, that ye may be able to stand against the wiles of the devil.

Ephesians 6:11 KJV

Being a warrior does not mean that you are not afraid at times. But you do it afraid. When a soldier is sent out to fight, he is afraid but he has been trained to push past his emotions and do what is commanded of him if he intends to stay alive. Soldiers train for months and years to go to war. They learn strategies to defeat their enemies. Like that soldier, you cannot fight a battle in your everyday strength. First, you must recognize that the fight is not carnal, it is spiritual.

For though we walk in the flesh, we do not war after the flesh: (For the weapons of our warfare are not carnal, but mighty through God to the pulling down of strong holds;) Casting down imaginations, and every high thing that exalteth itself against the knowledge of God, and bringing into captivity every thought to the obedience of Christ;

2 Corinthians 10:3-5 KJV

When something like cancer hits you or your family, you must realize that it means war and you are now a frontline soldier. Yes, you may be afraid, but you fight. You have to bring your thoughts under the obedience of Christ. You find your armor, you suit up, and you go to battle.

In my journey with cancer, one day after ministering in Hot Springs, Arkansas for a few days, still dealing with the diagnosis of cancer and still in some shock, I headed to my appointment to meet my oncologist and to hear the results of my CAT/PT scan. My biggest fear was that the cancer had spread to other areas of my body, which would move me to Stage 4 terminal. The night before, the pastor and the church prayed for me that I would be healed and continue to do what God had called me to do.

As I drove and prayed, I heard the Spirit of the Lord say, "When you get there, you say that I did *that*."

"Okay, God," I thought. I will do that. I thanked God that the results of the scan would be good. The closer I got to the doctor's office the more reality started sinking in, and I knew I was going to have to buck up and be a big girl and face this with faith. I got to my appointment, and I waited to meet my doctor. My heart was pounding out of my chest. My nerves were everywhere, but as afraid as I was, I thought, "God you are my strength."

My oncologist walked in the room. My heart pounded severely in my chest. The battle was very real at that moment. It was like having a gun pointed at your face and hoping they don't pull the trigger. My doctor was a young fireball. She introduced herself and asked how I was doing. She began to share with me the aggressive nature of the cancer that I was facing.

She said, "I am going throw everything I got at you." Then in that moment, she said, "And your CAT/PT scan looks good, and the cancer has not spread."

As she began to talk about the treatment, before she could get any further, I said, "Praise the Lord, Jesus did *that*!"

She looked at me and smiled and went on with the treatment plan. I don't know about you, but at that moment when I spoke those words, I had to pull from that part of me and use my faith and do what God instructed me to do in the face of the enemy, afraid. Not that the doctor was my enemy, but the demonic was there. When the Bible tells us not be ashamed of the Gospel, it's talking about those moments when it's not easy. But you must be obedient, operate in faith, and speak the truth in front of the world that may not believe like you. You do it afraid and trust that God has you.

She carried on with the treatment plan, but honestly, I didn't care about the treatment and how tough it was going to be. I was just thrilled that the cancer had not spread. My faith at that moment was built up, and I thought, "I can do this." I believe that because of my obedience in that moment proclaiming that Jesus was bigger than cancer caused a release of blessings and favor that would be bestowed upon me in the weeks and months to come in my journey called cancer. Let me say it again: Do it afraid!

Friend, be obedient in the battle. Look at it this way: God is the general and has a strategic plan for the battle that you are in and you must follow it if you want to win. You are going to have to quiet your mind and listen to your spirit, which means that you will need to feed your spirit man more than you feed your flesh. You will have to turn the television off, get off Facebook and other forms of social media if they are stealing your time and your mind, get rid of all negativity including negative family members and friends, and get in God's Word. You are going to have to know who God is and what God is to you in your situation. Every day, you must consult God to learn what He requires of you. If you skip any portion of the plan that God has, it could cause you to take a step in the wrong direction which will get you hit by the enemy and cause a setback or possibly get you killed. You need to surround yourself with faith-filled people who will not allow you to quit, and will not speak against the plan that God has you on to ride it out. You cannot be around people who will pity you. Pity pats, compassion moves. Pity will kill you. Compassion will point you in the right direction and give you the ability to fight. You cannot be around people who feed you negativity or people who pull you from the things of the Lord. In a battle, you have to stay focused. You cannot afford to hang out in non-productive things.

Watch for distractions. Getting distracted can open a door for the enemy to sneak up on you while you are unarmed and take you out. The devil wants you distracted. He will use all kinds of traps to get you off course. He will use people to distract you and get you off course because he knows if he is successful, the distraction can keep you from your Word. Then in the midst of your battle, you might doubt what God's Word says. The devil will try to pull you into unbelief, and at that point he will kill you spiritually, which will lead to a physical death. Friend, never attempt to take the devil on in your own strength. He will destroy you. He's been around for a long time. He is cunning and smart. He has studied you for years, and he knows your weaknesses better than you do. That is why it is so important in a battle to make sure you stay armed with the things of the Lord and that you know who God is in your situation. When you are armed with the Word of God and know that God goes before you and that the battle belongs to the Lord, your faith will remain intact; you will have the devil trembling.

The battle is real. It can be overwhelming if you look at it through natural eyes. It may appear that there is no way to win. But I am here as walking testimony that you can win. Today as I write this, I am cancer free. I had to ride it out with the Lord even when I was afraid. I had to walk it out the way God told me to. I had to prepare myself for battle. You will need to do the same. Get your armor on. Get your sword (the Word of God). Know who goes before you. Know who God is in your battle. Build your faith daily and keep it moving until victory is manifested and you have reached the other side.

CHAPTER 2

I CAN'T DO IT!

Have you ever been so scared that you literally could not move? You became petrified? I have dogs that stay in the house. Anytime there is a storm, I have this one dog, Scooby, that becomes literally petrified. He shakes and cries, and he has to be next to one of us. He hates storms and does not cope well. A storm or battle can do that to you. I remember one time after I had broken my neck, I was lying in bed. I believe it was a Saturday afternoon. My family went to Springfield, and I went to sleep. I had a vivid dream; you know, the kind that stays with you. I dreamed there was this man in a black suit with a very white lifeless face sitting at the end of the bed. He looked at me with piercing eyes that seemed to grab the depths of my soul, and he said, "You know I was sent to kill you?"

I tried to wake myself up, but could not get myself to wake up. Then all the sudden I heard a dog barking, and I immediately woke up. Scooby was looking at the end of my bed where this demonic being had been sitting in my dream, and he was barking. I immediately called a friend of mine who is a pastor, and without hesitation, he began to pray with me, and that fear, that petrified feeling, began to leave me.

I rebuked that dream or whatever it was and said, "NO! I WILL live and not die. You cannot have me."

The devil will try to throw everything and the kitchen sink at you to get you into fear over your situation. He wants you to say, "I can't do this." He wants you to think it's completely impossible, that there is no way out. He wants you without hope so that you will curl up and die. Not only do you need to know who God is, but you need to know who your adversary is and how he operates. Any good soldier studies his enemy and learns all about him, including his strengths and weaknesses. The problem with a lot of Christians is that they talk a lot about the devil but have not a clue who he is.

Satan knows the Word of God better than you do. He is cunning and smart. Never underestimate who you are dealing with. Satan can hear your words and read your actions.

To say things like, "This headache will be the death of me," says that you don't know your adversary.

That would be like a soldier in the midst of his enemies saying, "I don't have one weapon on me at the moment. Can you wait until I find one?" But we do that kind of thing all the time while being unaware of who is lurking to destroy us and our families.

> *The thief cometh not, but for to steal,*
> *and to kill, and to destroy...*
> John 10:10 KJV

So why give the devil the rope to hang you with? The problem with most people is that they live in a state of fear because they allow the enemy to keep them there. I can testify to that myself. I knew back in February that something was wrong with my body. I should have gone for my mammogram then, but I hesitated. Finally, driving home one day, the Spirit of the Lord checked me and said, "Go to the doctor tomorrow. Do not wait." That was in August, six months later! My battle might not have been so great if I had just listened to my body and trusted that no matter what, God was bigger.

We don't go to the doctor because we fear what he might say. We don't pay our tithes because we fear we will not have enough money for the rest of the week or month. We don't want to learn something new because we are fearful that we will fail. We don't talk to people for fear of rejection. The list goes on.

I remember when I was in high school, I wanted to try out for the cheerleading squad, but because I was not picked in junior high, I refused to try out in high school. My decision was based on fear of rejection. If you look at your own life, you will find that that you operated in fear concerning situations and things in your life which kept you from moving forward in that area, and in some cases, you let your fear cause you to just give up. The fact was that I had cancer. I had to face it. But the truth was, according to the Word of God, I was already healed.

Fear is the opposite of faith and can be just as powerful if given the opportunity. I remember the very first day I walked into the oncology department for my first round of what would be sixteen rounds of chemotherapy.

I thought to myself, "I am a little scared at the moment. What if I get sick? What if I can't do it?"

What if? What if? What if ... filled my mind. I was looking at my situation and the disease that was trying to overcome me instead of the solution and the One who was making a way of escape for me. I was allowing fear to trample all over my faith. If I wasn't careful, fear was going to petrify me. But I thank God that before starting this journey called cancer, I had been living in the Word of God for years, and because of that, the Word of God came flooding out of my heart. All the sudden, Scriptures like Philippians 4:13 came up in me,

I can do all things through Christ which strengtheneth me.

and Psalms 91 that says,

*"Because he loves me," says the Lord, "I will rescue him;
I will protect him, for he acknowledges my name.
He will call on me, and I will answer him;
I will be with him in trouble,
I will deliver him and honor him.
With long life I will satisfy him
and show him my salvation."*
Psalm 91:14-16 NIV

What looked impossible to me was very possible to God.

The Bible tells us in Psalm 23:4 KJV:

*Yea, though I walk through the valley of the shadow of
death, I will fear no evil: for thou art with me;
thy rod and thy staff they comfort me.*

We must either take the Word of God for what it says at face value, or doubt it. We need to stop thinking that maybe it means this, or maybe it means that. God, although complex, is very simple. Look at it like this: Cancer is death. So, I could say the above Scripture like this, yea though I walk through the valley of the shadow of death-cancer, I will fear no evil (that means any side effects that would try to come upon me through chemotherapy) for you are with me. I just made that personal to my situation. The Bible says I don't have to fear cancer because God is with me.

To get past the "I can't do it," you must make a decision to believe in God's Word. You must confess the Word over your life. We are affected by words, both those we hear and those we speak.

> *Death and life are in the power of the tongue:*
> *and they that love it shall eat the fruit thereof.*
> Proverbs 18:21 KJV

Have you ever been around someone who was negative all the time? When you left their presence, you felt negative. Some people are so full of doubt and unbelief that the atmosphere around them is dark. Remember the lyrics of that children's song? *Be careful little tongue what you say.* We think of it as just a children's song, but there is much truth in it. Words create an atmosphere. Therefore, when you are battling, you must keep the Word of God close to you and on your lips.

> *He sent his word, and healed them,*
> *and delivered them from their destructions.*
> Psalm 107:20

You've got to meditate on the Word of God. Make it personal to your situation. Study it to the point that you can believe without a doubt when you read Scripture like Exodus 23:25 (NKJV) that says:

> *So you shall serve the Lord your God,*
> *and He will bless your bread and your water.*
> *And I will take sickness away from the midst of you.*

You don't worry about what it looks like in the physical because you know that God's Word is true and if He said it, so be it, and that settles it. The Word of God says you can do it. It's not too difficult if you allow God to be the general in your battle.

> *Therefore I say to you, whatever things you ask when you pray, believe that you receive them, and you will have them.*
>
> Mark 11:24 NKJV

Really, that is very simple, yet we make it hard. It is sad to me that in this day and age we have Christians running around unaware of what God's Word has to say to them. I have asked people when they asked me to pray about a situation, "Well, what scripture are you standing on?"

They answer, "I don't know."

You will not be able to believe God for anything if you are not applying His Word to it. Your prayer is not effective because you are not standing on anything biblically.

Let's look at Mark 11:24 for a minute and break it down. First, it says, *Whatever things you ask when you pray.* Well, in my situation I asked for complete healing. Next, it says, *believe that you receive.* So, I asked for complete healing when I prayed. I had to believe that I received that complete healing. Here is where we mess up as Christians. This Scripture is about faith and if you do not understand faith, you do not understand God. Let me simplify it for you. Faith is simply putting your belief into action. What do you believe? Well for me, I believe God is my healer and that I am healed.

What do you do when you pray, and nothing happens? Well, let's look at this verse again. It does not say that when you pray, you should believe that it will manifest right at that moment. It says *when you pray believe that you receive.* That says to me that I am gonna have to ride it out for the moment. So, when I wake up every day, what do I do? I say, "Thank you, God. You are my healer. I thank you that your healing power is running through my body. I thank You that cancer does not reside in my body." Now, I may still see signs of cancer are still there in the physical, but I believe that I receive my healing and I am gonna walk it out until it completely manifests in the physical. I won't stop pursuing until I see the end result I want. God said healing is mine so why would I believe anything different? Again, what is impossible to man is possible with God.

Side note: We have a tendency to pick up what doesn't belong to us. What do I mean by that? I mean that God is not the author of sin. He is not the author of sickness and disease. The devil is. So why as believers are we picking up things from the devil? They don't belong to us. Give them back to him and take up your inheritance from the Lord. That is what belongs to us. The Bible tells us long life belongs to us. We are joint heirs with Christ, what is His is ours. We shall live and not die. The report of the Lord belongs to us. Stop claiming things that don't belong to you.

Mark 11:24 is just one of many Scriptures that we must understand and apply to our lives. All too often as a minister, I see people run to the altar wishing that when the man or woman of God lays hands on them, something miraculous will happen at that moment. They are looking for physical manifestations to magically happen right then and there, and when they walk back to their seats, they are disappointed because they didn't feel anything. Look, just because you don't feel it does not mean that a transfer didn't took place. Your faith and God's power placed together is the place where miracles happen. Your request was answered. You must believe that when you prayed that you received what you requested. Ride it out. Walk back to your seat with a smile thanking God till that thing comes to pass. As soon as people get it, they lose it because they don't see or feel something. But God does not operate in the emotional or feeling realm. God operates in the spirit realm. Don't be discouraged. If you come in faith believing you will receive what you desire, you will. Just keep praising and thanking God, and that thing will come to pass. Remember there is nothing impossible with God. Your situation did not throw God off the throne. Cancer did not make God nervous.

I remember when I got my first job as a paralegal. I was from a small town with a small-town mentality. I really thought I was stupid and not that bright. The lawyer I worked for was an older man who saw something in me that I could not see in myself. He disliked the word *can't*. I walked into his office with a document he asked me to work on, and I said, "I can't do it."

He looked at me, pulled his glasses down on his nose and said, "*Can't* is not a word. Just say you *won't* do it." I looked at him completely confused because I was sure *can't* was a word. Then he looked at me and said, "If you try hard enough, you *can* do it. Maybe you will fail once or twice but you will figure it out, and you can do it. When you say *I can't*, you are giving yourself an excuse to be less than, or saying you don't have the ability to do something. But I know you do have the ability."

He went on to say that maybe you have to try harder than someone else, but you can do it. I never said that word in front of him again. I took that document back to my desk and worked on it all day. I figured out how to do it, and I can tell you that I felt accomplished when I finished it. I learned a valuable lesson that day that became part of my motivation to keep moving no matter what adverse situation I faced. I may fall down sometimes, but I dust myself off and keep going even when I want to quit. If you decide you want to quit at something, don't say you *can't*, just say you *won't*.

I did not want to battle cancer. And yes, my initial reaction was, "I can't do this." But after the emotion lifted and I could see clearly, I realized I didn't have a choice. I also realized that if I was going to face cancer, then that must mean that I was strong enough to do so. I realized that who lived in me was way bigger than cancer. I began to feed my spirit man with the Word of God. I stopped saying, "I can't," and I started saying, "I can, and I will win." I did everything that I knew would irritate the devil and please the Lord. I became a warrior. Was it an easy fight? No way! Hardest journey I have ever been on in my life. But I am still here and still winning.

Your battle may seem too hard and you may not be able to see in the natural how you can do it, but regardless of what your brain is telling you, you can. I have met people who have beaten cancer not once but three or more times. I have met people who had lost everything and didn't have a clue how they were going to put food on the table, yet today they own department stores. I have met people who have lost children, and instead of agonizing and being demoralized, made it their mission to push for salvation for every unsaved person they could. You see, you can! You are stronger than you realize. You are a warrior. So soldier, get your war paint, your sword, and some faith-filled soldiers in your circle, and you will get to the other side of it, and you will win.

CHAPTER 3

TO KNOW HIM IS TO HAVE FAITH

But without faith it is impossible to please Him, for he who comes to God must believe that He is, and that He is a rewarder of those who diligently seek Him.

Hebrews 11:6 NKJV

Who is God to you? Who is God in your situation? Do you believe that what God does for someone else, He will do for you? These are questions you need to have settled in your heart (your spirit) when you are in a battle. You need to know who God is. The nature of God. You need to know who God is in your situation. And you need to believe that what God will do for someone else, He will do for you. To doubt or not firmly know the answer to any of these questions will result in defeat.

Who is God to you? Who is God to me? Well for me God is my everything. I learned years ago that without God I would surely die. I would not have made it through a rape or being molested as a child. I would have become an alcoholic. My life would have been drastically different. God is my source. At one point in my life, being accepted by people was far more important to me than being accepted by God. I valued what others thought of me more than I valued what God thought. But today, I value God's opinion way more than I value man's opinion. I realize that people will fail you but God never will. And I realize that the only way I am going to get through a situation, a storm, or a battle in this life is knowing who my Heavenly Father is and having a relationship with Him.

> *But without faith it is impossible to please Him, for he who comes to God must believe that He is, and that He is a rewarder of those who diligently seek Him.*
> Hebrews 11:6 NKJV

Let's examine the above verse. The first part of the verse says that it is impossible to please Him (God) without faith. So, what does that tell us? It tells us that emotions don't please God, good deeds don't please God. It says that faith pleases God. When God says that something is possible, that means it is possible. We must walk by faith and not by sight if we want to be pleasing to the Lord. This is a faith walk, my friends. Everything that we accept or do with God is by faith. When you got saved, you got saved by faith through grace. Ephesians 2:8 tells us that. Faith activates grace. Believing is a matter of faith. If you believe you are saved, you are activating your faith.

Let's look at the second part of Hebrews 11:6. It says, "…for he who comes to God must believe that He is…" Believe He is? He is what? Creator of the universe? Yes, we can say that. But let's take it a step farther and make it personal. It's a MUST that we believe He is Savior; He is Provider, He is a Waymaker, He is Healer, He is able, and so on. So now we can say it like this: For *me* who comes to God must believe that He is (my healer). Your faith should be rising at this point. I know I must have faith to please God. Simply, faith is putting your belief into action. And I know that I have to believe that He is what I need Him to be in my situation.

Now, let's look at the last part of Hebrews 11:6. It says, "… and that He is a rewarder of those who diligently seek Him." Let's look at the word *diligently*. Webster's definition of diligent says: characterized by steady, earnest, and energetic effort (www.webster.com/definition/diligent). God rewards those who diligently (steadily, earnestly, energetically) seek Him. Let me explain how this verse came into play toward my healing. I realized that was impossible to please God without faith, and that to acquire that kind of faith in God, I needed to study and meditate on the Word of God. I needed to speak the Word out loud so that I could hear it and it would build my faith. I also needed to know God in my battle. I needed to know Him as healer. I studied healing and how God dealt with sickness and disease. I got to know Him as healer. And because I was diligent in seeking Him, He rewarded me with healing, good health, and long life. See how that works? I needed to be a doer, not just a hearer of the Word. If you are not a doer of the Word, then you really don't have any foundation because you have never applied what you have heard. Smith Wigglesworth said, "If you wait until you need faith to get it, you're too late."

In a battle, you must have faith in God. You have to know Him in your situation, and you have to seek Him. God cannot be the last *go to*. He must be the first. He is the general in your fight. He understands and knows your enemy well. He will guide you into proper strategies, and give you the advantage, even when you face the battle afraid.

In August 2016, I was sitting in a workshop on worship. I wasn't honestly paying attention because my mind was on the biopsy I was going to have the following Monday. I was trying my best to concentrate but to no avail. The instructor was teaching on worship, and suddenly shifted to a personal testimony. He began to share about how years ago he had knots on the back of his head. They hurt and gave him headaches and bled at times. He went to the doctor but he already knew what it was. He said he was fearful of cancer. He shared about how the doctor told him it was skin cancer and that they would need to do radiation and possibly surgery. He said he told the doctor that he would just try Jesus first and if that didn't work, then he would come in and do what the doctor wanted. He said during this time, he remembered going outside to a tree and telling God that He would either heal him or he would be coming to see him. He rode it out for eighteen months believing that God's Word would not return void. He had to know God as his healer. He went back to the doctor after he knew he was cancer free, but just wanted confirmation of the fact, and the doctor confirmed what he already knew. But the doctor told him that the lumps were still there. He said that he got in his car and asked God why the lumps were still there. He said God told him they were still there to remind him of what He did for him. Praise the Lord! He said that when you see him rub the back of his head, it is because he is remembering what God brought him out of.

As the speaker told this story, at first, I wondered why he switched gears in his presentation. Then I realized that it was for me. He had no idea I was getting ready to go in for a biopsy, but God knew. God was encouraging my faith from the beginning for this journey. He was placing a testimony right in front of me that He is God, and what He did for the speaker, he would do for me. At that moment, God reminded me that I needed to know Him. God knew I needed to build my faith. I was about to face a battle that would require me to know my general (God), activate my faith at a much deeper level, and know my enemy. In my last book, *For Such a Time as This*, I talk about not missing your God moments. This was a God moment. God shifted that instructor's gears because I needed to hear that testimony. My mother died of ovarian cancer when she was only fifty-eight years old, and she was a faith-believing evangelist. God knew that when that diagnosis came, I would think of her outcome and be fearful that it would also be my outcome, so He placed someone in my path to show me that you can win a battle with faith even when you are afraid.

Could the instructor have walked that journey out for eighteen months without knowing who God was in that situation? Without having faith in an unseen God but knowing that He was already healed? I don't believe so. He could ride that storm out because he had faith in God and he knew who God was to him. I have spoken to him since, and yes, he was afraid amid the battle, but he knew that God was bigger than cancer. Friend, that is why it is so important that you do not wait until the storm blows in and knocks you out of the boat. If I had never believed that God could heal me of a cold, do you know how much harder it would have been to believe that God would heal me of cancer? All too often as Christians, we wait to read the Bible. We wait to praise God. We wait to worship. We wait to pray until we have a major need. Why do we do that? Because we have no relationship with Him and we don't really know Him.

Not only did I need to know God as my healer. I needed to know Him as my provider. We did not have insurance, so I studied Scriptures pertaining to finances. Now let me say this: If you don't tithe and you are not a giver into the Kingdom of God, you are robbing yourself of blessings. You need to start. If you can't live on one hundred percent of what you make now, then ten percent is not going to make that much of a difference. God's heavenly economy defies understanding because ninety percent goes further than one hundred percent when you tithe, and one hundred percent will never be enough when you don't tithe.

> *"Will a man rob God? Yet you have robbed Me!*
> *But you say, 'In what way have we robbed You?'*
> *In tithes and offerings. You are cursed with a curse,*
> *For you have robbed Me, Even this whole nation.*

> *Bring all the tithes into the storehouse,*
> *That there may be food in My house,*
> *And try Me now in this," Says the Lord of hosts,*
> *"If I will not open for you the windows of heaven And pour out for you such blessing That there will not be room enough to receive it. "And I will rebuke the devourer for your sakes, So that he will not destroy the fruit of your ground, Nor shall the vine fail to bear fruit for you in the field," Says the Lord of hosts;*
> Malachi 3:8-11 NKJV

But as I started to know Him and develop a much deeper relationship with Him, I trusted what He said to do in the fight. One night as I was laying in my bed, just thinking about the whole thing I was getting ready to face and the financial burden it was going to put on my family, God quickened my spirit to give away ten books. The next day I posted on Facebook that I was giving away ten books. I ended up giving away close to one hundred books! Within two weeks, we received a letter that a foundation decided that we met financial qualifications and that they were paying for the four doses of a drug I needed TOTALLING $60,000! That's God! Let me tell you how I know that is God. We don't meet any financial qualifications, but with God all things are possible. Then within a week of receiving that letter, we received another letter stating that seventy-five percent of all hospital bills and fifty percent of all clinic visits would be taken care of. Again, that was God! Next, we received a check in the mail from the hospital, which made me laugh because we owed them money. Another foundation had come in and paid for another drug I had to take totaling about $16,000 more. Do you see how God works? When you operate by faith, it pleases the Father, and He operates on your behalf. He rewards those who diligently seek Him.

About a month prior to surgery, I had a dream that when they opened me up, there would be no cancer and that the tumor that remained would not be cancerous either. I told my husband and best friend about this dream. When I went in for surgery, I had one tumor remaining out of the three. It had shrunk down dramatically but was still there. When the pathology report came back, it showed that I was completely cancer free. Jesus did that! That tumor did not have cancer. Today I am in remission and living by faith to remain cancer free.

Lots of people make the mistake of thinking that once their manifestation happens that they can go on living as before. No, my friend, you must *maintain* a lifestyle of faith. You cannot afford to fall back, and honestly, why would you want to? Maintaining your faith and relationship with our Heavenly Father is so much easier than trying to beg God for something or living in worry and fret. Think of faith like this: It's like any parent. When you tell your children that you will do something for them, you expect them to believe you. They don't see what you will do in the physical at the moment you tell them, they just believe you to do what you say you will do. When my children got sick at a young age, I told them they would be alright, and they believed that they would be alright because Mom and Dad were their protectors and they believed that we would never allow anything bad to happen to them. Well, that is really all faith is about. God expects you to believe what His Word says. The difference between Him and earthly parents is that He cannot lie. His Word is true. You can bank on that.

CHAPTER 4

ROW, ROW, ROW YOUR BOAT!

Row, row, row your boat
Gently down the stream,
Merrily merrily, merrily, merrily
Life is but a dream

(From The Franklin Square Song Collection, 1881, New York)

Warning: Not for the faint of heart!

Cancer! It's from hell. From the moment that you are diagnosed and hear that word, the battle to get to the other side is on. You can't cave at any moment or you will sink! It's not for the faint of heart. You wake up every day and say, "Even though my body hurts, even though I want to quit, I gotta keep rowing. I gotta get to the other side."

Cancer tries to steal your identity. The treatment given to kill the cancer also kills every good and bad rapidly-growing cell you have, which means side effects that you never saw coming. Side effects that include losing your hair that you love to hate to fix, but wish it was still there so you could fix it. Treatment causes rashes on your face and body and makes it difficult to eat. Your eyebrows and eyelashes disappear, and your eyes water because they are so dry. When you get the strength to look in the mirror one more time (because you feel like the walking dead), you keep rowing to the other side. As your fingers and toes go numb and the nails fall off, you keep rowing to get to the other side. Some have short battles and some have long battles. Regardless, the battle is still big no matter the length of the fight.

Your mind is a constant battlefield. You face the fact that you are in a mortal body that can die. You fight thoughts of leaving your children and your family. Your mind fights against you at times. Cancer will try to pull you to dark places. It attempts to steal your will to live. But you dig deep down to the depths of who you are. You find a place you have never pulled from before and you find the strength to keep rowing to the other side. When you cannot sleep and rest seems so far away, you keep rowing because you have to get to the other side. Even though you are surrounded, you feel all alone, but you keep rowing to get to the other side. One more treatment. You say, "I can do it." NO! You must do it. When they are wheeling you back for surgery, and the thought crosses your mind that you might not wake up, you do it because you have got to get to the other side. When you wake up and the pain is more than you can bear, you keep rowing because you have got to get to the other side. When you can't stop throwing up because you are violently sick at your stomach after surgery, you keep rowing to get to the other side. When you see that you have drains that hang off you after surgery that cause discomfort and pain, you can do it, because you have got to get to the other side. Knowing that you will have permanent numbness in your back of your arm because they had to cut through a nerve, you keep rowing because you have got to get to the other side. And when you look in the mirror for the first time after surgery and you realize that the breasts that God gave you are forever gone, and you will be forever changed, you keep rowing because you have got to get to the other side. When you are at the darkest moment, and it feels you've seen a small glimpse of hell, it is then that you understand what it means to hold on to your faith; it's all you've got. But it's all you need.

How do we get to the other side? Let's look at Mark 4:35-41 NKJV says,

> *On the same day, when evening had come,*
> *He said to them, "Let us cross over to the other side."*
> *Now when they had left the multitude, they took Him along in the boat as He was. And other little boats were also with Him. And a great windstorm arose, and the waves beat into the boat, so that it was already filling.*
> *But He was in the stern, asleep on a pillow. And they awoke Him and said to Him, "Teacher, do You not care that we are perishing?" Then He arose and rebuked the wind, and said to the sea, "Peace, be still!" And the wind ceased and there was a great calm. But He said to them, "Why are you so fearful? How is it that you have no faith?" And they feared exceedingly, and said to one another, "Who can this be, that even the wind and the sea obey Him!"*

In Mark 4, we see that Jesus was in a storm. It's interesting to me because in this story, Jesus shows us what to do when we are in the midst of the storm. We see Jesus wanted to go the other side after He had preached to the crowd. Then all the sudden a big storm approached. The storm wanted to keep Jesus from going to the other side and perhaps even kill Him. Side note: Anytime you speak faith, you speak the Word of God, the devil will come at you. The devil comes to steal the Word of God from your heart. If he can do that, he can cause you to doubt and operate in fear, then he can kill you. Some of you are thinking right now that you will just not speak the Word. You're thinking that if you do not operate in faith that the devil will leave you alone. Well friend, in that case, he will leave you alone because he already stolen the Word from you and caused you to believe a lie and put yourself in a downward spiral. You are already in the enemy's camp when you stop speaking the Word of God over your life.

Back to the boat. Jesus had just finished preaching to the crowd and said, "Let's go to the other side," and then He went to rest. The key word here is *rest*. What is rest? Merriam-Webster Online Dictionary defines rest as "peace of mind or spirit" and at rest as "freedom from anxieties." I find it interesting that even the world sees rest as freedom from anxieties and peace of mind and spirit. Jesus was resting. He did not have a care in the world. He had peace in His mind and spirit. Then all the sudden a storm blew through. The storm did not wake Jesus. The water smashed against the side of the boat and filled it, but it did not wake Jesus.

Jesus reminds me of my husband, who could sleep through anything. A tornado could blow through the house and he would not wake up. Jesus was resting, and He was fully confident that He would be okay.

What woke Jesus? The doubting disciples saying, "Master, don't you care if we drown?"

Sounds like us, doesn't it?

"God, don't you care that I am in this mess?"

"God, don't you care about all this coming down on me?"

"God, I am battling cancer. Aren't you concerned?"

God's answer is basically, "No, I don't," or "No, I am not." It's not that He doesn't care or have compassion. He does. He is just is not concerned about the plot or the ploy that is against you. He knows He is fully capable of handling the situation. He is not concerned what people think of you. You see, Jesus did not care what people thought of Him. He was not distracted by trying to please people like we are. The Bible says He knew the thoughts that man had toward Him. He was not moved by their plots and ploys. He knew where His help came from. We need to not be concerned about people pleasing either. If you are worried about what someone thinks of you, you are placing your faith in that person and not in God. Jesus was only concerned about pleasing the Father. When we are concerned about pleasing God, we will not be moved by people pleasing, and we will always operate in compassion. Jesus was fully confident that everything would be okay and that they would get to the other side. He is equally confident that you will too if you operate in faith according to the Word of God.

We see in Mark 4:39 that Jesus woke up and rebuked the storm by saying, "Peace be still." He then looked at the disciples and said (in modern vernacular), "Guys! Why you afraid? You still don't have faith?"

Even after Jesus calmed the storm, the disciples still said, "Who is this man?" They still had no idea that the man in the boat was the One that could calm any storm that they would ever face.

We can be like that. God calms a storm, we move to the other side, and then we say, "How did that happen?" It happened because God was in the midst with you fighting for you.

We can be afraid (and believe me, I understand that). Battling cancer gave me moments of fear and anxiety. The more fear and anxiety I had, the more I prayed and built my faith by getting in the Word.

In Mark 4, Jesus showed us how to ride out the storm. While He was in the storm, He rested. The Word went forth, then He got in the boat, and He rested because He knew He would be alright. We have to learn to rest in the Lord. Speak the promises of God in your situation, then rest. I had to speak the Word of God over myself and then rest. No warrior can fight twenty-four hours a day, seven days a week. The only one who can is God.

The Lord will fight for you, and you shall hold your peace.
Exodus 14:14 NKJV

When you speak the Word of God over your situation, be like Jesus, and rest. Let's not be like the disciples. Don't stay in your emotions. I will be honest and share that going into surgery gave me anxiety like no other. I kinda understand what Jesus felt like when He was in the garden the night before He was to be crucified. Now, I said *kinda*. You know Jesus was dealing with extreme anxiety because He was sweating drops of blood. He even said, "God, if there be any other way…"

Trust me, I also said, "God if there be any other way."

God could have sent a legion of angels to rescue Jesus, but the plan was to ride it out because the outcome was so much greater than the storm that Jesus was facing. Yet, in all of Jesus' emotions, He still said, "If it be thy will…" He knew that the biggest storm of all was brewing, and He knew He was going to have to battle, but He was getting to the other side and fulfilling the will of the Father.

At the beginning of my battle with cancer, God showed me how I was to ride it out. Let me tell you this: In any situation you face, go to God first. Listen to what He says to do. Don't be so quick to hear the words of man in your situation. Sometimes, church folks mean well but they can pressure you into doing things that were never intended for you to do, and you will fail miserably at it because you are pleasing man, not God. You will get discouraged in your faith because you will be thinking, "I did what they said. How come nothing has happened? Why is it getting worse?" Because you are pleasing people, and not pleasing God.

I had many people say, "Just trust God, you don't have to go through treatment. Just walk this out with God." Although that is the way maybe they walked it out, that was not the way that God showed me. There are many ways that God has for us to get through storms. Don't be ashamed of where you are or where your faith is. God loves you, and He wants you well in all areas of your life.

Church can be like high school with peer pressure. When man's words, contrary to God's leading, were spoken to me, I smiled and went home and said, "God, I will do this the way You show me and I will close out all other voices." I knew my faith was not at a place where I could just walk it out without treatment, surgery, or medical intervention. And that was okay. I wasn't too proud to say, "God, this is where I am."

As I walked it out the way God said, my faith rose to levels I never knew where there. Today I am cancer free. I was cancer free when they operated on me. See, I rode it out the way God said, and as I did, God put the right doctors in my path, sent me to the right hospital, and gave me the right nurses. Every door was opened without me having to struggle to get them to open. My faith was continuously encouraged because I was in the will of the Father for my situation. He was building my faith. When the boat was filling with water, I rested, and He got me to the other side. He placed the right people in my path to encourage my faith, people who never caused me to doubt the direction I was going. So, friend, fight the way God says.

Ride it out the way God says. Don't people please because it will kill you. Be a God pleaser. He will give you rest and peace in your mind while the storm is raging all around you, and He will show you how to get to the other side.

The mistake that cancer makes (or any other battle that Satan tries to defeat you with) is that it creates warriors. Warriors in faith! They are bloodied, scared, and they know how to fight. They know where to pull from. They have been in the boat when the water was crashing against it and filling up, so they know exactly how to ride it out. They know who is in the boat with them. They stand firm, take a deep breath, and say, "I know the Master of the wind. He is in the boat with me. Whom shall I fear?"

You can learn a lot from a warrior. If you're in the boat and the storm is raging and you can't get to the other side, pray that God places a warrior in the faith in your path. He or she will show you and give you the tools to get there! Whatever you are facing, speak the promises of God in that situation, then rest. Rest your mind, rest your body, and rest your spirit. Jesus is in the boat. Ride it out. And never ever forget - God is fighting for you!

CHAPTER 5

PRAISE IS A WEAPON – USE IT!

> *But at midnight Paul and Silas were praying and singing hymns to God, and the prisoners were listening to them. Suddenly there was a great earthquake, so that the foundations of the prison were shaken; and immediately all the doors were opened and everyone's chains were loosed.*
>
> Acts 16:25-26 NKJV

Praise is a weapon, and in a battle, you must know how to praise the Lord.

When I was diagnosed with Stage 3 Triple Negative Breast Cancer, I can honestly tell you that praise was the last thing on my mind. I'm just real. I was afraid and had doubt. My anxiety was at the point that I had to take something just to sleep. My heart pounded wildly, I got dizzy, and could not think clearly. Cancer has a demonic force attached to it and if allowed the opportunity, it will kill you. My mom went home to be with the Lord after her fight with ovarian cancer. I took her to every medical appointment and chemotherapy treatment. I sat with her in the hospital and sang praises unto the Lord. As I would walk into the doctor's office or hospital with her, I sang and spoke praises. It wasn't until I was hit with cancer and walked into the oncologist's office as a patient that I realized that the fight is way different when you are the one having to battle it. At that moment I remember saying, "Okay God, it's me and you in this fight. I thank you in advance that I am healed. I will walk this out how you want me to no matter how afraid I am. I will praise you, and I will not stop. You are my Father who loves me, and You are bigger than cancer."

I thought about Paul and Silas and how horrible it must have been in that prison shackled and locked in. Prisons back then had to be horrible. Dirt floors, nowhere to go to the bathroom; the smell had to be dreadful. But Paul and Silas looked beyond their situation and prayed and praised the Lord. Even if they were afraid, they spoke no fear. They did not complain, they just praised and prayed. And at midnight look what happened! The earth shook so hard it caused the prison doors to open and the chains to be loosed, not only for them but for the others who were in that prison. When I think about this story, I can't help but get excited! The Bible says that the other prisoners heard them praying and praising. I can't say for sure, but I believe they were saying, "Yes Lord, what they said," and began to praise and pray right along with Paul and Silas. Praise out of the mouth of one who believes influences the surroundings even if there are adverse circumstances. Your praise can be so contagious that it causes others around you to want to praise God as well. Your praise can be so effective that it causes chains to fall off others. Be a praiser, not a complainer!

Let's look at the Levites:

> *And when he had consulted with the people, he appointed those who should sing to the Lord, and who should praise the beauty of holiness, as they went out before the army and were saying: "Praise the Lord, For His mercy endures forever." Now when they began to sing and to praise, the Lord set ambushes against the people of Ammon,*

Moab, and Mount Seir, who had come against Judah;
and they were defeated.
2 Chronicles 20:21-22 NKJV

Just like Paul and Silas, when they began to praise the Lord, He showed up on their behalf. Praise is a weapon in battle.

You may be saying, "Well, Roxanne, that sounds great, but I am unsure about what praise is and how to praise God."

Well, let me start by saying this: If the only time you think you are to praise God is in church, you are wrong. I am a worship leader, and as a worship leader, I see this all the time. Praise and worship are not taught in the church today like they should be. It appears that people and some pastors think that it only applies to Sunday services as a prelude to the Word being spoken. NO! It's not just a church song service. That is a very small portion of praise. Praise should be on your lips continually. The Bible commands all living creatures to praise the Lord. (Psalm 150:6).

One Hebrew word for "praise" is *yadah*, meaning praise, give thanks, or confess. Another word often translated to the word "praise" in the Bible is *zamar*, which means to sing praise. Another word translated "praise" is *halal* (the root of *hallelujah*), meaning to praise, honor, or commend. As you can see, the purpose is to give honor and thanks to the One who is worthy of praise. I'm sure that you can think of something every day to give honor and thanks to the Lord.

We should praise the Lord simply because He is Lord! There should be times we praise the Lord out of love and honor. God has given us praise to combat the enemy of Christians. Praising God puts the devil to flight. Praising God lifts your faith and reminds you and all those around you that God has dominion and power over creation.

There are many Scriptures that tell us to praise and acknowledge the power of God:

Let the redeemed of the Lord say so,
Whom He has redeemed from the hand of the enemy,

Psalm 107:2 NKJV

Redeemed means delivered or set free.

Christ has redeemed us from the curse of the law,
having become a curse for us (for it is written,
"Cursed is everyone who hangs on a tree"),

Galatians 3:13 NKJV

Christ set us free from the curse or bondage of sin and Satan.

They shall utter the memory of Your great goodness,
And shall sing of Your righteousness.

Psalm 145:7 NKJV

You know David said, "while I live will I praise the Lord…" (Psalm 146:2). He remembered the great and wonderful goodness of the Lord, and it caused him to praise the Lord!

I love the book of Psalms. It is a beautiful collection of songs filled with worship and praise to God. When I was young, I read Psalms and Proverbs over and over because I loved how Psalms was written. You can sing the Scriptures, and Proverbs had short Scriptures that I could memorize easily. Sometimes, I find myself singing a Psalm during the day. Get the Word of God buried in your heart so that you can do battle. You can open Psalms and confess it with your mouth and go to battle. Praise is a weapon.

Praise unto God is a holy undertaking. Praise is a spiritual event. There is power in praise. Here are four aspects of praise to consider:

1. Praise elevates your faith:

Praise is faith in action. When there seems to be nothing else you can do, you can stand before God and offer up a sacrifice of praise. Even though your circumstances in life look bad or even hopeless, your heart is breaking, and your mind does not fully understand, you praise! As you begin to magnify and minister unto God and talk about how great He is, your faith becomes stimulated.

Praise provides an antidote for worry. Do you worry? Wouldn't it be nice if we could take a pill and never worry again? I would be first in line. But there is an antidote, a substance to counteract the poison of worry. Worry is poisonous. It kills your faith and builds strongholds in your mind. Worry builds a picture of defeat, failure, and lack of confidence in God. So, we counteract that picture with praise. Praise drives out the poison of worry and builds confidence back in us to trust and believe God who is able.

David knew that. He did not worry about what God said He would do for him. That would have been doubt. Instead, he praised God for what He said He would do. Some people need to begin to praise God instead of begging God. Whatever the situation may have been, David said, "Oh that men would praise the Lord for His goodness…" (Psalm 107:31 KJV). If your faith is wavering, start praising God. Go to the Book of Psalms and read how David praised God, and stay with it, then watch God manifest Himself in your situation.

2. Praise releases your hold and acknowledges God as the One who wins the victory:

Praise always leads to triumph. Praise in the middle of a "prison" experience becomes faith in action. Praise becomes the key to opening the door to whatever binds you.

> *And I will give you the keys of the kingdom of heaven, and whatever you bind on earth will be bound in heaven, and whatever you loose on earth will be loosed in heaven.*
>
> Matthew 16:19 NKJV

One of those keys is praise, which is the language of faith.

> *And he said, "Listen, all you of Judah and you inhabitants of Jerusalem, and you, King Jehoshaphat! Thus says the Lord to you: 'Do not be afraid nor dismayed because of this great multitude, for the battle is not yours, but God's. Tomorrow go down against them. They will surely come up by the Ascent of Ziz, and you will find them at the end of the brook before the Wilderness of Jeruel.*
>
> *You will not need to fight in this battle. Position yourselves, stand still and see the salvation of the Lord, who is with you, O Judah and Jerusalem!' Do not fear or be dismayed; tomorrow go out against them, for the Lord is with you."*
>
> *And Jehoshaphat bowed his head with his face to the ground, and all Judah and the inhabitants of Jerusalem bowed before the Lord, worshiping the Lord. Then the Levites of the children of the Kohathites and of the children of the Korahites stood up to praise the Lord God of Israel with voices loud and high.*

So they rose early in the morning and went out into the Wilderness of Tekoa; and as they went out, Jehoshaphat stood and said, "Hear me, O Judah and you inhabitants of Jerusalem: Believe in the Lord your God, and you shall be established; believe His prophets, and you shall prosper." And when he had consulted with the people, he appointed those who should sing to the Lord, and who should praise the beauty of holiness, as they went out before the army and were saying:

"Praise the Lord, For His mercy endures forever."

Now when they began to sing and to praise, the Lord set ambushes against the people of Ammon, Moab, and Mount Seir, who had come against Judah; and they were defeated.
II Chronicles 20:15-22 NKJV

The people of Judah, Jerusalem, and King Jehoshaphat released their hold and acknowledged God as their help. Praise becomes your mightiest weapon in the battle because God becomes your main focal point. You allow God to bring about the victory instead of trying to do so yourself. The Bible tells us in II Chronicles 20:15 that the battle is not ours, it is God's battle.

There are times when we get tired in the battle and even in our walk with the Lord. But we must never allow our praise to fall off our lips, never stop praising God. Praise brings victory. It lifts our eyes from the battle to the victor and the victory. I remember going through treatment. I had to have sixteen rounds of chemotherapy. That is a massive amount of poison flowing through my body. Doctors gave me a chemotherapy that they called the *red devil* (part of a three-part chemo regimen known as ACT, which stands for Adriamycin (red devil), Cytoxan, Taxol. It causes hair loss, short term memory loss, nausea, loss of appetite, stomach pains, loss of sleep, sweats, mouth sores, watery eyes, neuropathy, and other side effects. You wouldn't wish it on your worst enemy. Having to deal with cancer and treatment was horrifying enough, but then they gave me a treatment that they called red devil? I had to have four rounds of that stuff. It was very aggressive chemo and had major side effects, heart attacks being one of them. I quoted Psalm 91. Especially Psalm 91:10-11 KJV that says,

There shall no evil befall thee,
neither shall any plague come nigh thy dwelling.
For he shall give his angels charge over thee,
to keep thee in all thy ways.

The other Scripture that I quoted was Exodus 14:14 NKJV which says,

The Lord will fight for you, and you shall hold your peace.

Some days were harder than others. Some days I wanted to wave the white flag. But even in my weakest moment, I released my hold, and I praised. On one particular week, I believe I had two more treatments left, and I became very tired, not just physically but emotionally and spiritually. I cried all week long. My mouth tasted like glue and metal and was extremely dry. Food was disgusting to me. My eyebrows thinned out pretty good that week, and I developed a chemo rash on my face. I lost seven pounds. It just wasn't my week, to say the least. I remember thinking that I didn't want to do this anymore. I just wanted to go home. As I thought that, immediately in my spirit my favorite Scripture rose up:

I can do all things through Christ who strengthens me.
Philippians 4:13 NKJV

I started to speak that Scripture out loud. I rose up and began to praise God in a whisper, and before I knew it, I was praising God with my hands lifted and could hear myself saying, "No matter what this feels like or looks like, I will praise You! I will exalt your name! You are fighting for me! I won't quit or give in! Satan, you are a liar!" I encouraged myself like David. I got up and carried on. Friend, don't quit. Even afraid, even when you're weak, you can open your mouth and praise. It's food for your spirit.

3. Praise ushers in the supernatural power and presence of a supernatural God into your situation:

Read II Chronicles 14:9-15. What a powerful message to weak, struggling people!

Then Zerah the Ethiopian came out against them with an army of a million men and three hundred chariots, and he came to Mareshah. So Asa went out against him, and they set the troops in battle array in the Valley of Zephathah at Mareshah. And Asa cried out to the Lord his God, and said, "Lord, it is nothing for You to help, whether with many or with those who have no power; help us, O Lord our God, for we rest on You, and in Your name we go against this multitude. O Lord, You are our God; do not let man prevail against You!"

So the Lord struck the Ethiopians before Asa and Judah, and the Ethiopians fled. And Asa and the people who were with him pursued them to Gerar. So the Ethiopians were overthrown, and they could not recover, for they were broken before the Lord and His army. And they carried away very much spoil. Then they defeated all the cities around Gerar, for the fear of the Lord came upon them;

and they plundered all the cities, for there was exceedingly much spoil in them. They also attacked the livestock enclosures, and carried off sheep and camels in abundance, and returned to Jerusalem.

Praise always gives God His rightful position in your life and in the church. Paul and Silas sang praises unto God, and God responded by a supernatural earthquake. When I was in the early stages of my treatment, I had only two treatments of the infamous red devil chemo. My oncologist wanted to check me to see where the tumors were after a few treatments. I had three. One tumor was seven centimeters, one was five centimeters, and one was two centimeters. My doctor began the exam, and to her amazement, the tumor that was seven centimeters was a little over one centimeter, and the one that was five was at one centimeter, and we could not feel the tumor that was previously at two centimeters. Jesus did that! That's supernatural! I praised God continually. Even when the enemy attempted to instill doubt, I did not listen, I praised. At times, I had to look straight ahead and not listen to the voices that were trying to discourage me. Praise was on my lips.

As an individual, praise is an important part of your walk with God and is a crucial weapon against the enemy. As a church, praise is a must. As we join together in one accord and praise God out of true hearts, we take our place as priests, and the cloud of the Lord, His glory, will fill the place.

God is Spirit, and those who worship Him must worship in spirit and truth.
John 4:24 NKJV

We shall say as David said in Psalm 59:16-17 NKJV:

But I will sing of Your power;
Yes, I will sing aloud of Your mercy in the morning;
For You have been my defense
And refuge in the day of my trouble.
To You, O my Strength, I will sing praises;
For God is my defense,
My God of mercy.

4. Praise glorifies God

The words we speak let others, including the host of spiritual beings, know that we give God all the glory. Glorifying God should be our lifestyle. It shouldn't be an afterthought, but a priority, especially when we are in the midst of a battle. The Bible says that the Lord is good and His mercy endures forever (Psalm 136:1 NKJV).

Psalms 107:32 NKJV says,

Let them exalt Him also in the assembly of the people,
And praise Him in the company of the elders.

When we as believers come together, we must praise the Lord. That is how miracles take place. God is worthy of our praise and praise brings great benefits to those who actively praise the Lord. You will never get to the other side of the storm or defeat the enemy without it.

Remember that praise is a weapon. Get up and praise Him!

CHAPTER 6

BATTLE BUDDIES

The storm is raging all around you. It feels like the enemy is about to close in on you. You are tired and weary. You say, "God, I just don't think I can carry on much longer." Then out of nowhere appears a friend. But this is no ordinary friend. This friend goes far beyond having a cup of coffee with you. This friend has faith and strength. This friend is a *Battle Buddy*.

Everyone needs a faith-filled friend, a battle buddy. When the waves come crashing in, and you have rowed till the twelfth hour and are about to give up, a battle buddy says, "Hold on, I will row for you while you rest." They never speak negativity to you or against you because they know words have power and they see the storm and battle you are in. Battle buddies speak life into the atmosphere, and they know how to encourage your faith. They will never allow you to quit.

The Bible gives many accounts of battle buddies. Poor Job didn't have faith-filled friends. Instead, he had friends who questioned his walk with God, and insinuated that Job did something to bring his calamities upon himself. Job's wife, who should have been his biggest battle buddy, instead told him to curse God and die. Job remained faithful to God, however, and was given double blessings for his trouble. I am sure it was not easy for him while surrounded by doubt and fear to remain constant in his faith. He is the exception to the rule.

David and Jonathan were battle buddies.

> *Now when he had finished speaking to Saul,*
> *the soul of Jonathan was knit to the soul of David,*
> *and Jonathan loved him as his own soul.*
> I Samuel 18:1 NKJV

Jonathan sacrificed for David.

Naomi had Ruth. In Ruth 1:16-17 NKJV:

> *But Ruth said: "Entreat me not to leave you,*
> *Or to turn back from following after you; For wherever you*
> *go, I will go; And wherever you lodge, I will lodge;*
> *Your people shall be my people, And your God, my God.*
> *Where you die, I will die, And there will I be buried.*
> *The Lord do so to me, and more also,*
> *If anything but death parts you and me."*

Ruth saw Naomi in trouble, and she was there for her. She was self-sacrificing.

Elisha attached himself to Elijah.

> *Then Elijah said to him, "Stay here, Elisha; the LORD has*
> *sent me to Jericho." And he replied, "As surely as the LORD*
> *lives and as you live, I will not leave you."*
> *So they went to Jericho.*
> 2 Kings 2:4 NKJV

Elisha was devoted to his friend, his mentor.

Moses had Aaron in one of the greatest partnerships we find in the Bible. Sometimes God will call you to the work of another. We receive friends, but sometimes we are called to be a friend to another. Aaron gladly spoke for Moses. Because of their willingness to work together, they became one of the greatest stories in the Bible.

These are just a few examples of people who were *ride-or-die* individuals. Going through the journey called cancer, there were many times that I became weary and emotionally tired. But God surrounded me with battle buddies, ride-or-die people to encourage me at my weakest point. God sent people who were fearless in their faith, people who told me they would pray and who actually did pray, people who canceled things on their schedule and missed work to be there for me in my time of need, people who put aside what they were going through in their own lives to be a faith-filled battle buddy for me, people who refused to let me quit.

See, you cannot afford to have doubters, complainers, fault finders, gossipers, or any type of negative people or negativity in your mist when in a battle. You need people who will be faithful like Jonathan was to David, who are willing to lay down their lives for you. You want people like Aaron who will hold up your arms when you are too tired to do it.

Job had a tremendous amount of faith, and his so-called friends could not sway him from his God, but some of us are not equipped like Job. If people around you are always causing you to doubt who you are and what you believe, then you need new friends. You need friends who will do it afraid with you.

I remember when I first started chemotherapy. I woke up one day, and it was like there was a wall in my mind. I knew what was past the wall but for some reason, I could not reach the other side of the wall. I couldn't remember things, and my mind was dark and foggy. I sent a message to a group of friends and asked them to pray for me because I felt like I was under attack. Immediately, one of them called me, and she said, "Oh no, you're okay, that is chemo brain." She began to explain what was going on. Then she prayed for me. Immediately, my mind cleared up, and anytime that happened again, I spoke against it. She did not cause me fear. She did not say, "Well, you are gonna go crazy." She simply explained what was happening, calmed my storm, and prayed. She was a battle buddy. She was also the friend who went to treatment with me. She was a retired nurse, which helped, but she never placed fear in me with her medical knowledge. She prayed over me before the chemo entered my body. She did not care who was around or heard her. She just battled with me.

It always helps when you live with a battle buddy. My husband allowed me to have moments when I fell apart but he refused to let me stay there. He constantly said, "I don't know what it is like to go through what you are going through, but you are strong, you can do this. Just think how God is going to use this to help others." He motivated my faith continually. He wasn't like Job's wife, thank God!

Battle buddies know how to correct you if your thinking has gone a little left. They never insult you but move you into the right way of thinking. My best friend knows me well. She can correct me without me taking offense. We need people like that in our lives. We all go a little left at times, and we need honest people who love us enough to say, "Get yourself together and stop it." What we don't need is someone constantly telling us how wrong we are and that we will never amount to anything, or constantly feeding us negativity.

I love the story of Peter.

> *Peter answered and said to Him,*
> *"Even if all are made to stumble because of You,*
> *I will never be made to stumble." Jesus said to him,*
> *"Assuredly, I say to you that this night, before the rooster*
> *crows, you will deny Me three times." Peter said to Him,*
> *"Even if I have to die with You, I will not deny You!"*
> *And so said all the disciples.*
>
> Matthew 26:33-35 NKJV

You know Peter loved Jesus very much. He cut off a soldier's ear in a battle for Jesus. But the enemy caused great fear in Peter and caused him to deny his mentor, his friend. Although he thought he was a battle buddy, when push came to shove, he really was not, and Christ knew it. It did not mean that Peter did not love Christ, he did. He just could not press past his fear and do it afraid for his friend. Lots of people are like Peter. We love our friends, and we say things like, "I would do anything for you," but the reality is that most people will not.

In the Garden, Jesus went to pray. He was about to face the biggest battle of His life. He took Peter and the two sons of Zebedee with Him and asked them to stay and watch with Him. But guess what? He found them sleeping. They could not give Him one hour. Their flesh was weak. Battle buddies stay in the fight. They know how to control emotions and do what is necessary for you. Poor Peter just could not conquer his flesh. He was a friend, but honestly, he did not know how to be a battle buddy.

Battle buddies fight to the death for you, and are willing to rearrange their lives for you. I thank God for my battle buddies, my faith-filled friends who know how to fight. Cancer is a Goliath. It took a team of believers to conquer that giant. But today, I stand here cancer free. I thank God for keeping me even when I was afraid. I thank God for my friends that at times I know were in fear but never placed that on me as they continued to fight for me. They never allowed me to quit. They would have laid their lives down for me at any given moment.

It is in the midst of a battle, in the midst of a raging storm, you will find out who your faith-filled friends are and who they are not. A battle will always show you who will stand with you and who will not. We need to learn to be faith-filled friends to other people. There is a saying that goes, "Not all your friends are for you." That's very sad. It is hard to accept that some people who call themselves my friends really are not. Unfortunately, it is true. Sometimes people befriend you to get what you have, jump on your coattails, or find out information. Sometimes people hope for your demise in the midst of a battle and smile right in your face. I had some of those. I knew who they were. I smiled right back and kept it moving. Sometimes the enemy will place people in your path to distract you so that you are not focused on the storm up ahead. Pray for discernment. Get your spiritual antenna up. Jesus did. He knew who was for Him and who was against Him, but He kept it moving and did the will of the Father. God will bring people in your midst who are the Jonathans, the Ruths, and the Aarons that you need, exactly when you need them. If you are reading this and saying, "I don't have any friends like that," then friend, start praying them in. They will come.

Sometimes you will meet battle buddies in the midst of your battle who are genuinely concerned and praying for you, people who will encourage your faith. They may be seasonal people, and they may become lifelong, faith-filled friends. They may only appear in your life when the storm is raging, but you know that you can count on them.

In closing, appreciate those people that God places in your life that are battle buddies. Never take them for granted. I thank God every day for my battle buddies, my ride-or-die friends. They love me for me. They ask nothing of me other than to be with me. My defeat over cancer did not come alone. I had many battling buddies that were for me, praying and believing with me that I would win this war. Pick your close friends wisely. There is a saying that goes, "Keep your friends close and your enemies closer." I say, "Rebuke your enemy and keep your battle buddies close!"

CHAPTER 7

WINNING! THE BATTLE IS IN THE MIND

I've missed more than 9000 shots in my career. I've lost almost 300 games. 26 times, I've been trusted to take the game-winning shot and missed. I've failed over and over and over again in my life. And that is why I succeed.

Michael Jordan

*A champion is afraid of losing.
Everyone else is afraid of winning.*

Billie Jean King

*What winning is to me is not giving up,
is no matter what's thrown at me,
I can take it. And I can keep going.*

Patrick Swayze

Boom, crush. Night, losers. Winning, duh.

Charlie Sheen

*I have fought the good fight,
I have finished the race, I have kept the faith.*

Paul in II Timothy 4:7

I woke up from surgery, and after dealing with the pain and nausea, I had to deal with the emotional trauma. I went home and was fairly quiet. My best friend, JoAnna, stayed with that weekend because my husband had to take my daughter to dance competition. I had a bilateral mastectomy, which is the removal of both breasts, along with the start of reconstruction, the hardest thing I have ever been through in my life.

For the first few days I just really didn't look. I didn't want to, and I was afraid. I already felt that I looked like the walking dead, and now I was going to have to face seeing what happened to my body. After about four days, I finally did it afraid and looked in the mirror. As I type this right now, I am crying. I can tell you I cried and cried and continued to cry. I almost couldn't recognize myself. I had to battle my mind. I had to deal with depression, fear, and anger. I was so mad. I felt like this was completely unfair. My mind shifted back to when I was young and I felt ugly and rejected. I became vulnerable and somewhat insecure. I couldn't sleep and got sick over it. Every night that I refused to face it head on, depression began to put its grips in me.

One night I sat on the end of my bed and said, "God, you surely did not bring me this far to let me drown now. You wouldn't allow me to face this if I was not strong enough with You to face it."

*For God has not given us a spirit of fear,
but of power and of love and of a sound mind.*
II Timothy 1:7

I had to get my mind under control. It took me days to come to terms with it, but one day I faced it. I stared at myself in the mirror and I realized that the devil is a thief who comes to steal, kill and destroy (John 10:10). What I was seeing was a fact, but the truth is that just like Job, God was going to restore what cancer had taken from me.

> *And the Lord restored Job's losses*
> *when he prayed for his friends. Indeed the Lord*
> *gave Job twice as much as he had before.*
> Job 42:10 NKJV

To conquer the very thing that the devil sent to take you out, you must face it and maintain a good attitude. I truly believe that half my battle with cancer was keeping a good attitude right from the start. The devil comes at you through your thoughts. He places a thought in your mind and hopes you fall for it. That is why you don't want to stay in the unknowing too long because the battle is in the mind and the mind has a great big imagination. When terrified, it can cause you to believe all kinds of lies. You'll be up all night googling everything under the sun. You will be on social media airing out your dirty laundry even though that is the worst place to air out dirty laundry. When the enemy is waging war, get your armor on and get in the ship because you got to get to the other side.

Quitters never win. I have never met a successful person that did not try and fail at least once. I have met unsuccessful people who have never tried because of fear. To win and obtain a victory means that you are going to fall once or twice. You may take a hit here and there, but you don't stop, you don't quit. While battling cancer, I made up my mind to get up and face another day and, therefore, I was one step closer to winning. Victory would soon be mine.

You cannot win if you never confront the very thing the devil is trying to take you out with. Being afraid causes you to operate in fear and fear will keep you in the unknowing. The unknowing is dark, and it is a torment to the mind. It's the devil's playground, and no one wins except the devil. That is why knowledge is power. Once you confront the thing, you will find that it is not as scary as it appeared. Cancer was a scary diagnosis, but it was not as scary as I had it in my mind to be. If I never confronted the cancer that was attempting to steal my life, it would have won.

The key to winning is always keeping your mind centered in on Christ, staying in your Word, and praising the Lord all the way through, especially during the battle.

Maintaining the Victory

To truly win you must maintain an attitude of victory even after the manifestation comes. With my healing, I must maintain my faith walk to remain healed. Many times, what happens to believers is that they get the victory and as soon as they get it, they lose it. Why? Because they forget to keep walking it out. They forget to keep making right confessions. Don't forget the place God brought you out of. Maintain your walk daily.

Watch your words. How does your mouth contribute or hinder the outcome of the trial or testing you are going through? Your words set the atmosphere. Develop an attitude of victory daily. Here is an example: A shoe company sends a sales representative to another country to evaluate whether it would be a good idea to sell shoes in that country. The sales associate calls back and says, "Cancel all production, they don't wear shoes here." The CEO decides to get a second opinion and sends another sales associate. The sales associate calls back and says, "Start production immediately, no one here has shoes." Always obtain and keep an attitude of victory. We don't rejoice because the baby is sick, the bills are not paid, the car will not start, or the job is over, but we keep a consistent confession of victory before us. We rejoice rather than predict bad news. The Bible tells us that life and death are in the power of the tongue.

God made us in His image, and gave us the ability to rule or dominate circumstances in our lives. We can bring about curses or blessing by the same method He used to create the world: by our words. You can maintain your victory by speaking life to the situation daily. Jesus pleased the Father because He lived by faith daily.

If every day you wake up and face the world with the right attitude and faith in God's Word, you are winning, regardless of how it appears to you in the physical. I went into a battle called cancer. I was afraid. I fought a tough fight, and when the water was coming in the boat and I thought I might sink, I remembered who was in the boat with me. When I was tired, I rested. God was fighting this battle for me. I praised when it looked bad and I praised when it looked good. I put my armor on and continued. As a result, today I am cancer free and healthy. God wants us here to build His Kingdom. I say it like this, "I don't have time to die." And friend, neither do you. You might be afraid, but ***Do It Afraid*** and as you do, God will build your faith, and you will say like me, "WINNING!"

A TESTIMONY: SARA TOMA

DO IT AFRAID

The most difficult words I've ever had to swallow were, "You have cancer." At first, I was devastated with my diagnoses of breast cancer, but the love, prayers, and support brought me back to the true nature of the Lord. This process has not been easy, but I've met a lot of wonderful people throughout my cancer journey; each helped show me how fragile life is and that God's love conquers all. One lady stands out from the rest; she was my main inspiration through all this. I met Roxanne Potter in the infusion room on my third and most difficult treatment of chemo. She was already halfway through her treatments, so she had firsthand insight. I was in so much pain that day, and she could relate to it. She reassured me I would get through it all. She never pushed her belief of God on me; but just watching how she handled herself and how joyful she was given her predicament spoke louder than words. I thought, "Wow! How can this lady be so happy while facing such a challenging time in her life?" Her attitude ignited the spark that I needed to get closer to God; it is intangible to describe how it feels when God's presence is noticed; the wonders of the mind start to become clearer. I realized God was with me all along and it wasn't until I acknowledged Him that things started falling into place. I picked up the Gospel after many years and for the first time, every word resonated with me. My past experiences, the people I've met along the way, and my reason for existence started to unfold before my eyes. I felt I was being guided not by my gut but by the Holy Spirit. The more I read the Word and prayed with my whole heart, the more God proved His presence to me. I do not doubt for a second that God brought Roxy and me together during this time in our lives. She not only prompted me of God's holiness but she encouraged me to lead by example. She gave me the courage to conquer my fears and build confidence in God's purpose not only for myself but for others. I am truly thankful for my pink soul sister; she brought me closer to my Savior which brought me closer to peace. God knew I needed someone like Roxy to remind me of the importance of spreading our joy no matter how challenging life gets, for when we emit joyfulness, we shine with purpose and God's truth. Roxy taught me how to demonstrate that with grace, no matter what, for there is always someone who can benefit from how you carry God's love.

ABOUT THE AUTHOR

 Roxanne Potter, originally a paralegal for fourteen years, has also been in ministry, either part time or full time for over twenty-seven years. She is the facilitator of *For Such A Time As This* women's conferences and retreats. She is an ordained minister through DCM Ministries, worship leader, songwriter, author, and evangelist. She is an active member of Mount Calvary Powerhouse Church in Poplar Bluff, Missouri. She has directed a faith-based restoration home, led worship, and spoke in many venues. She holds cowboy churches during big-barrel racing events.

Roxanne is happily married to Donnie Potter and has three beautiful children: Jake, Stone, and Josie. They own a quarter horse farm in Mount Vernon, Missouri, and are active in the sport of barrel racing. Roxanne is also a Triple Negative Breast Cancer Warrior. She loves the Lord and has a strong desire to see people set free to walk in the freedoms given to them through Jesus Christ.

Note from the Publisher

Are you a first time author?

Not sure how to proceed to get your book published?
Want to keep all your rights and all your royalties?
Want it to look as good as a Top 10 publisher?
Need help with editing, layout, cover design?
Want it out there selling in 90 days or less?

Visit our website for some exciting new options!

www.chalfant-eckert-publishing.com

www.ingramcontent.com/pod-product-compliance
Lightning Source LLC
Chambersburg PA
CBHW071456070426
42452CB00040B/1548